Zodiac Relationship Guide

The Ultimate Guide on Zodiac Sign Compatibility

Table of Contents

Introduction

I want to thank you and congratulate you for downloading the book, *"Zodiac Relationship Guide"*.

This book contains proven steps and strategies on how to understand sign compatibility.

Each person is born under a sign. Some people say that this sign has a way of affecting people's characteristics. These unique and individual energies are very important to consider when it comes to love.

Most people are already familiar with the Sun Sign compatibility and use it as guide in love. Many people find themselves being attracted to people that they do not really understand. Using astrology to find romance or to understand your partner's characteristics can be very helpful if you wish to build a lasting relationship.

Learning about your sign can give you an insight on how you can draw love into your life. Venus is a great influence when it comes to finding love. The goddess acts as a muse which can lead people towards their ideal mate. Venus in a person's personal chart can tell a lot about how they would approach love and relationship with others.

Thanks again for downloading this book, I hope you enjoy it!

The trademarks that are used are without any consent, and the publication of the trademark is without permission or backing by the trademark owner. All trademarks and brands within this book are for clarifying purposes only and are the owned by the owners themselves, not affiliated with this document.

Chapter 1 The Zodiac

Early astrological systems were used to predict more practical things such as the weather and the seasons. Every ancient culture has their own story about the heavily bodies. Stars and the moon became the symbol for divine beings and planetary movements were interpreted as a heavenly sign. During this time, astronomy and astrology were the same. Ancient astronomers would record patterns in the sky and use it to interpret life experiences.

Astrology has been practiced for thousands of years. Astrology has been used to predict the future and to understand cosmic phenomena. Astrology can also help people look for a suitable partner based on their zodiac sign.

People's signs are determined by the Zodiac constellation at the time of their birth. There are twelve signs in the Zodiac and each of them has their own characteristics. These signs can be grouped into four elements- fire, water, air and earth. Water signs include Cancer, Scorpio and Pisces. These signs are the epitome of emotion and sensitivity. Fire signs like Aries, Leo and Sagittarius are linked to leadership and enthusiasm. Air signs such as Gemini, Libra and Aquarius tend to be intellectual. Earth signs such as Capricorn, Virgo and Taurus symbolize practicality.

Most astrological reading is based on personality types. A full professional astrological reading can be extremely detailed and can show how certain elements and interactions can affect you. This reading is much applicable when it comes to zodiac love compatibility.

Chapter 2 Aries (March 21- April 20)

Aries are described as curious and energetic individuals. They often want to get involved in different activities rather than become a spectator. Their constant need for excitement can push them into new territories and help them experience new things.

Aries Men

Aries men are greatly influenced by the planet Mars. They like to move through life at their own pace. This can make them very exciting but other people also have a difficult time keeping up with them. If you want to attract an Aries male, you have to be clear that you are interested in him.

How to attract:

- Aries men are highly enthusiastic and often look for adventure. They also love surprises since it can keep them mentally engaged. Predictable activities often bore them.

- Display some self-confidence. Aries men don't usually like shy women. They find confidence very sexy and attractive.

- Antagonize him slightly. Aries loves a good challenge. Try to take an opposite perspective on a certain topic. This will peak his interest and will challenge him to dominate the situation.

Aries women

Women under the sign of the Ram are very comfortable in their own skin. She has a very strong personality and has a very independent nature. These self-reliant women are often seen as an inspiration for other women.

7

How to attract:

- Make a bold move. Make her believe that you are strong enough for her.

- Act confident in the right way. An air of confidence does not require you to brag about yourself.

- Let her take the lead. Once she accepts your initiative, gently allow her to take the lead. This enables her to understand just how much you want her.

Best Love Matches

Sagittarius

Both Aries and Sagittarius are physically and mentally agile. They will enjoy challenging each other. Once these two fire signs meet, their passion can explode into large proportions. Sagittarius also enjoys adventure and often has great social skills that Aries finds attractive.

Aries

This is a dynamic match where people can feel as if they are looking in a mirror. A relationship formed between two Aries can be very powerful and rewarding.

Gemini

Both signs enjoy flirtations and both signs can give each other the room to grow. Gemini can provide Aries the excitement that he needs while Gemini can enjoy the Ram's loyalty.

Chapter 3 Taurus (April 21- May 21)

Taurus highly values stability and solidarity. They also have the keen eye for aesthetics most especially when it comes to food. They can be carefree and sensual pleasures are very important to them.

Taurus Men

Taurus men have a subtle strength that women finds attractive. They are not known for their aggression and are very sensitive about their partner's nature. Taurus men are also known for their patience. Their protective nature is enough to make a woman feel safe. Taurus men are very picky and they often take a lot of time in deciding on a partner.

How to attract:

- Understand him. Taurus men have high standards with regards to woman and they can also be elusive. They are attracted to women who can respect their preference.

- Be open to a long term relationship. Taurus is not the type of man who would demand commitment immediately but as he opens up to his partner, he would want someone who would stick around for a long term.

- Show that you are reliable. Taurus men do not like too much risk. Avoid giving them too much surprise since this can make them very nervous.

Taurus women

Taurus women are not easily upset but can be very stubborn when pushed to the limit. Taurus women are emotionally strong and can survive a lot of challenging situations. They are also very loyal and expect the same from their partners.

How to attract:

- Take it slow. This is the golden rule if you wish to attract a Taurus woman. Coming on too strong can scare a Taurus woman away.

- Prettify yourself. Taurus is extremely romantic and is usually attracted to handsome men. Take special care with your grooming and wear clothes that suit you.

- Don't play too hard to get. Taurus women are uncomplicated. Do not spend time playing mind games with them.

- Demonstrate your practical skills. Material stability is important for Taurus women. Taurus women want a partner that is very practical and can handle financial matters easily.

Best Love Matches

Virgo

Virgo and Taurus are Earth signs that can form a sweet and old fashioned relationship rooted in hard work and shared values.

Pisces

Taurus ad Pisces can share a karmic bond. Taurus provides stability for a Pisces who can often be overwhelmed by worries. Pisces shares sensitivity and imagination for Taurus.

Capricorn

Capricorn and Taurus union is another Earth and Earth combination. Capricorn can push the relationship forward.

They can also share a very sexy partnership which only intensifies as the couple matures together.

Chapter 4 Gemini (May 22- June 23)

Gemini is represented by the Twins which can also explain their duality in nature. They can be very inconsistent about everything. People born under this sign often have the gift of insight. They are also good communicator and are usually very witty.

Gemini Men

Men born under the sign of Gemini are very energetic, intellectual and enthusiastic. They can be very fun but they tend to change their mind easily. A Gemini's wit and charm can leave a great impression on other people's minds.

How to attract:

- Be open to change. Gemini is always trying to look for excitement. He can quickly become bored so you have to be very good at creating a sense of excitement to keep him romantically involved.

- Flirt. Flirting is one of Gemini's best traits. Play a little hard to get and avoid coming to earnest or desperate or he will quickly lose interest.

- Give him space. Gemini is threatened by people who try to tie them down. They value their freedom too much so avoid acting too possessive.

Gemini Woman

Gemini women are known for their vivacious spirit. Gemini likes to travel since it gives them the opportunity to visit different places and meet different people. These women are also intelligent and love to communicate with other people.

- Strike up interesting conversation. Gemini likes to flirt intelligently. They would rather talk about clever topics than celebrity gossip.

- Arouse their curiosity. Gemini cannot refuse intriguing things. Show her how unique you are and avoid following the crowd.

- Keep it casual. Gemini women like to take their time with love. Keep your affections light and playful and avoid intimacy too soon. Gemini is great at flirting and is usually attracted to men who like to take their time before committing into anything.

Best Love Matches

Libra

Libra and Gemini match can be very ideal. They both enjoy being intellectual who loves to socialize with other people. They also share the same love for culture, art and fun. Their relationship would generally be warm and open.

Aquarius

A love match between Libra and Aquarius is bound to be full of surprises. This can suit both Libra and Aquarius since they like spontaneity. Their mutual love of communication also ensures that they both enjoy a strong sense of friendship while maintaining a romantic relationship.

Aries

Aries and Gemini is both full of energy and vitality. Aries' leadership qualities can be matched by Gemini's ingenuity. They will also enjoy their mutual love of knowledge and learning.

Chapter 5 Cancer (June 22-July 22)

Cancer is a water element Zodiac sign. They are known for being deep and emotional. Their need to love evokes sentimental thoughts. They also have the habit of holding on to their past and find it very difficult to let go. Cancer is deeply influenced by their emotions.

Cancer Men

Cancer men can be viewed as shy individuals who are very reserved but they will gradually open up to the people that they like. Cancer men are very affectionate and are thoughtful of other people's feelings.

How to attract:

- Avoid rejection. Cancer men are very sensitive and cannot handle rejection. They are often concerned on how people view them and they hate being embarrassed.

- Act helpless. One tip in attracting Cancer men is to act helpless. They like to act as your protector. Be sure to show them your vulnerable side too.

- Ask about their roots. Attract a Cancer's interest by asking about their family background. Remember that family is very important to Cancer. One way to make him fall in love you is to make sure that you create a good relationship with his mother.

Cancer Women

Cancer women can be passionate and stubborn at the same time. There is no certain pattern to this woman's mood swings. Cancer women also take time before trusting someone. They can become irritable but would not purposely do anything to hurt another person's feelings.

How to attract:

- Show her that you are the domesticated type. The ideal life for a Cancer woman is a life is having a nice house filled with adorable children. They can only commit to a person who can be with them in a long-term relationship.

- Be kind and caring. The female Cancer is reserved and shy and can be easily intimidated by strong personalities. Show her that you are kind and caring person who can sympathize with her.

- Appeal to her values. Cancer women are attracted to traditional values. She needs and wants a partner that can be loyal and faithful to her. She is much more impressed with genuine kindness than good looks.

Best Love Matches

Taurus

Taurus and Cancer share the same need for stability and security. Their differences can make up for the other's weakness. Both signs are family oriented and are sensitive to other's feelings.

Scorpio

Scorpio can be a difficult match for other signs but not with Cancer. Cancer's possessive nature can help make Scorpio feel secure while Scorpio's passion can encourage Cancer to come out of the shell more.

Virgo

Virgo and Cancer enjoy taking care of each other. They are also very good at communicating which can help their relationship thrive.

Chapter 6 Leo (July 23- August 23)

Leo is the most masculine sign of all the Zodiac signs. It often described as being powerful and majestic. They are born leaders and enjoy associating with people. Despite their strength, they are warm spirited and is driven by their desire to be loved.

Leo Men

Leo men are very lively and gregarious that it is quite impossible not to get affected by their personalities. They are well aware of their strengths and can sometimes make them lazy in approaching their goals.

How to attract:

- Flattery. Attracting a male lion is easy provided that you make him feel that he is the most wonderful man in the world. He loves to hear compliments and praises.

- Have good manners. Leo men are always in the company of others so they would want a partner who can socialize well.

- Allow him to take the lead. Leo usually assumes the dominant role in a relationship.

- Dress up. Leo loves to be admired and would also love to bask in the glory of others. He generally prefers colors such as orange and yellow.

Leo Woman

Leo women always need attention, admiration and respect. They can be viewed as arrogant and proud at times but they can also be generous and devoted. Behind a tough exterior,

Leo women are sensitive and like to treasure everything that she possesses.

- Go to parties. Leo women enjoy parties and like to be in the company of men who likes to be playful. She also likes to show off so avoid competing for the spotlight.

- Show her affection. Underneath their strong personality, Leo needs a lot of compliment to make them feel happy and secure.

- Make her a little bit jealous. The idea of a little competition will help ignite their passion and will make her fight to win your heart.

Best Love Matches

Sagittarius

Sagittarius and Leo both share a mutual love of freedom and adventure. They can encourage and inspire one another.

Aries

Aries and Leo have the same temperament. They can be energetic and passionate as long as they take care of each other's needs. Both signs also love physical intimacy and would make it a bonding point in their relationship.

Gemini

Gemini and Leo approaches life with enthusiasm. Leo's warmth can help dampen Gemini's cynicism while Gemini's cheerfulness can go well with Leo's natural joviality.

Chapter 7 Virgo (August 24- September 22)

People born under the sign of Virgo have a strong need to feel loved and needed. They are also very clever and detail oriented. They are very dependable and would never be the type of people to neglect their responsibility. Virgo is known for being overly critical of everything around them but this can also serve as a sign of great love and respect for their work.

Virgo Man

Virgo men tend to approach romance carefully and usually take a lot of time getting to know a person before pursuing a romantic relationship.

How to attract:

- Be a classic beauty. Like most men, Virgos are attracted to beauty. However, they prefer neat and classic looks over trendy fashion.

- Avoid messy displays of emotions. Virgo is not attracted to the 'damsel in distress' type of girl. They prefer women who share an analytical approach to life.

- Be honest. You won't attract a Virgo by pretending to be someone you are not. Try to be straightforward about your strength and about what is important to you.

Virgo women

Virgo women are loveable, intelligent and practical. They do have the tendency to become restless and cranky so they need someone who can help them stay focused.

How to attract:

- Ask for her assistance. Virgo women can become shy and passive so do not expect them to make the first move. However, avoid scaring her off by coming on too strong. A good way to attract her attention is if you ask for her practical advice. Virgo women love fixing things and cannot refuse a cry for help.

- Virgo can be a perfectionist so make an effort to look clean and presentable.

- Impress her with your common sense. Try to stay calm and collected since Virgo women are uncomfortable with emotional outbursts.

Best Love Match

Taurus

Taurus and Virgo tend to be introverts. They would enjoy being with each other's company instead of socializing at parties. Virgo's ability to pay attention to details can compliment Taurus's focus on security.

Cancer

Cancer and Virgo may share differences but they can suit each other well. Virgo's practicality can compliment Cancer's need for security. Cancer and Virgo are also very caring and love to dote on their partners.

Capricorn

Capricorn and Virgo are both hard-working and diligent individuals who place value on intellectualism. They also have the same outlook in life and can make a harmonious relationship together.

Chapter 8 Libra (September 23-October 23)

Libras highly value justice, fairness and peace. Just like other air signs, Libra is also very sociable. They also place a high regard to music and arts. When it comes to love, Libra is well matched with other air signs but can also get along with fire signs. Libra has a reputation of being unable to take a stand since they do not like to offend anyone. Their desire to please other people can lead them to dishonesty.

Libra Men

Libra men are loving and compassionate. They are considered as one of the most romantic men of the Zodiac. They are usually graceful and athletic at the same time. They also have a deep sense of loyalty and fairness.

- Do not be aggressive. Overly aggressive tactics can scare the passive Libra. You can win him over with pleasant conversation and cute smiles instead.

- Be romantic. Libra craves romance and likes a woman who can accept romance in return.

- Be social. Libra does not like to stay home night after night. You are most likely to attract him at a social setting where he feels more at ease.

Libra Women

Libra women are known to be elegant and attractive. They are very intelligent and courteous who can smooth any problem with diplomacy. They enjoy surrounding themselves with luxury.

How to attract:

- Dress to impress. Libra women like to be well-groomed men. Tailored clothes and neat appearance can immediately attract her at first glance.

- Be romantic and classy. Libra women like luxurious and romantic things. She will enjoy candlelight dinners and trips to art galleries.

- Flirt but do not be a pervert. While Libra girls like to flirt, they do not like verbal aggression and physical advances.

Best Love Match

Aquarius

Both Aquarius and Libra love to socialize with other people. Their life together can be very rich and rewarding. They will also enjoy sharing each other's pursuit. Libra's diplomacy can counteract Aquarius's stubbornness.

Gemini

Gemini and Libra can make a wonderful match. They perfectly suit each other socially, intellectually and sexually. They both have a wide variety of interest and are full of passion in everything that they do.

Sagittarius

A Sagittarius and Libra combination will never be boring. Libra can keep things interesting for the adventurous Sagittarius while Libra can benefit from the mental stimulation that Sagittarius inspires.

Chapter 9 Scorpio (October 24-November 22)

Scorpio is the most celebrated and feared among the Zodiac sign. Scorpio possesses a high degree of innate power. They are usually at their best if the situation allows them to change and transform. Despite their commanding nature, people born under the sign of Scorpio are very sensitive.

Scorpio Men

Scorpio men are very independent and will not let anyone tell them what to do. They are always focused on their goals. Scorpio men are also very attracted to power and position.

How to attract:

- Be mysterious. The best way to attract a Scorpio man is to create an air of mystery around you. He may find you more interesting if you reveal yourself slowly.

- Be upfront and truthful. Scorpio will unlikely fall in love with a person who has previously deceived him. Remember that these men are very intuitive and can figure out if you are being truthful or not.

- Stand your ground. Scorpio is attracted to strong minded people who have enough guts to get the things that they want in life.

Scorpio Women

Scorpio women are difficult to understand but they also love to meet people who can intrigue them. Scorpio women also like to discover their partner's personality and does not want it handed over to them.

- Never tell them what to do. Scorpio women are the type of girls that can hold their own ground. They also value their independence and are used to thinking for themselves.

- Be assertive. Nothing attracts a Scorpio woman than a man who is confident and is very bold in their actions. Avoid being soft and timid if you want to capture her attention.

- Don't play head games. Make sure to back all of your promises. They want a man who knows the difference between a game and a challenge.

Best Love Match

Cancer

Cancer and Scorpio share many differences but these diversity can complement each other. Scorpio's powerful nature can make Cancer feel secure and protected. Cancer's natural ability to please others can keep Scorpio's jealously at bay.

Capricorn

Capricorn and Scorpio make a good match. Capricorn's patience and diligence can compliment Scorpio's imagination. They also have a wonderful sexual chemistry.

Pisces

The dreamy Pisces has no problem allowing Scorpio to lead. Scorpio can also compensate for Pisces indecisive nature.

Chapter 10 Sagittarius (November 23-December 21)

Sagittarius is another sign that posses a dual nature. It is symbolized by half man and half animal. They can be energetic and optimistic who loves to be active. They like to travel and often engage in sports. They are best matched with fellow fire signs or some of the air signs.

Sagittarius Man

Sagittarius male are very positive and often have a bright outlook in life. They like to explore different things. They are very versatile and like to meet people from all walks of life.

- Be mysterious and aloof. Sagittarius is philosophical in nature and loves to solve puzzles.

- Be fun and playful. Sagittarians are happy people and they do not want to be with a gloomy girl. Try to engage them into small conversation and laugh at their jokes.

- Be unpredictable. Remember that Sagittarians can get bored easily so you have to work constantly to keep their attention.

Sagittarius Woman

A female Sagittarius is very independent, idealistic and loves to travel. They are also known to be flirtatious and playful. Sagittarians also have the tendency to be inquisitive and they have a philosophical approach in seeking the truth.

- Be unpredictable. Nothing can spark a Sagittarian's interest than an enigmatic guy. Being unpredictable provides an air of mystery that a Sagittarius woman wants.

- Be the prize. Sagittarius loves a good challenge. Make yourself the most eligible bachelor and make her win your affection.

- Respect her freedom. A Sagittarius is very independent and her partner needs to appreciate that. Avoid being clingy and give her enough space to grow.

Best Love Match

Aries

Aries and Sagittarius enjoy being social and would welcome any adventure. Their partnership will be full of joy and excitement. They are also both optimistic.

Aquarius

Aquarius and Sagittarius shares have the same attributes. They can easily have a strong and harmonious relationship. They also both thrive in change and adventure.

Leo

Leo and Sagittarius share a great love of freedom and adventure. They often see life and love as source of amusement and entertainment. They also share the same view about physical intimacy.

Chapter 11 Capricorn (December 22-January 20)

Capricorn in an Earth sign which means that they typically have a practical approach in life. They are described to be prudent, responsible and diligent. They also almost never refuse a good challenge. Capricorn natives like to receive a lot of recognition and they also like to feel useful. The recognition that they want is often material in nature and they like to be luxurious.

Capricorn Men

Capricorn men tend to be conservative and like to go by the rules. They can be seen as cold and detached but it is only their way of protecting themselves from pain. They can also be admired for their logical and rational thinking.

How to attract:

- Be sober. Try to stay calm and collected when you are with a Capricorn man. They do not like too much emotional outburst.

- Be friends with them first. Capricorns like to take it slow and they are more likely to fall in love with a person who became their friend first.

- Make him laugh. Capricorns can be very melancholy and stoic at times. They enjoy a person who has a good sense of humor. Despite their serious aura, they can enjoy a good joke about anything.

Capricorn Women

Capricorn women are very modest and goal oriented. They are also methodical and disciplined. They are the type of woman who knows their strengths and weakness. The

Capricorn woman seeks security and growth. They also have a dynamic way of dealing with challenges.

How to attract:

- Be a man of action. Capricorn women are not dreamy and romantic. They often do not have illusions about their romantic relationship. They are also more impressed by accomplishments you earned through hard work and perseverance.

- Be organized. Capricorns are good at organizing and do not like inefficiency. Remember that she likes things to go as smoothly as possible.

- Take note of their age. Capricorn women are like wine- they only get better with age. Young Capricorns tend to be very serious for their age while a mature Capricorn is more capable of being fun.

Best Love Match

Taurus

Taurus and Capricorns are Earth signs and tend to share the same perspective in life. They also place a great value in money and security. Taurus will appreciate Capricorn's diligence while Capricorn will benefit from Taurus' dedication.

Pisces

Pisces will benefit from the stability of Capricorn while Pisces can help Capricorn get in touch with their imagination. Each sign have the strength that can make up for the other's weakness.

Virgo

Virgo and Capricorn are very similar when it comes to their views on life. They both know how to work hard. Although this match cannot be the most romantic union, it has an excellent chance for a long- term success.

Chapter 12 Aquarius (January 21- February 18)

Aquarius loves new ideas and thrives on progress. They do not often fancy anything overly traditional and outdated. Aquarians are also great humanitarians and are open to ideas that can make the world a better. Aquarians are uncomfortable at showing too much emotion and they place a great value on their independence.

Aquarius Man

Aquarius is strong willed in their own way. They seek to learn the truth and they often find themselves involved with a lot of activities which occupy most of their time. They are also very imaginative and intelligent. Most Aquarians are soft spoken and courteous but they tend to rebel against norms.

How to attract:

- Be intellectual. They are often attracted to women who can start an intellectual conversation.

- Be yourself. Aquarians are highly attracted to anything eclectic. Any person who dresses, thinks or acts out of the box will intrigue an Aquarius female.

- Be passionate about life. Aquarians move from one idea to another and they find it difficult to stick to anything. They would like a partner that can inspire new ideas and passions.

Aquarius Woman

Aquarius women have enough inner power to conquer any challenge. These women know how to speak their mind but they also are unprejudiced about other people's opinion.

How to attract:

- Stand out from the crowd. It is very difficult for Aquarius to pin point the person they really like among the crowd so you will have to stand out among the rest if you wish to impress her.

- Don't tie them down right away. Do not try to pin down an Aquarius with any label right away. You have to be very patient try not to push your luck.

- Avoid emotionally charged discussions. This sign cannot deal well with emotional baggage. They also have a difficult time opening up to others.

Best Love Match

Sagittarius

Sagittarius and Aquarius are very energetic and vibrant. They also enjoy adventure and unpredictability. This pair loves to dream big and plan ahead for their future.

Libra

Libra and Aquarius likes to be around people and they both share the need to have an active social life. They also mutually appreciate arts, music and intellectual pursuit.

Gemini

Both Aquarius and Gemini are social individuals who like variety. This pair is also fun loving and adventurous. This union will rarely be affected by jealousy.

Chapter 13 Pisces (February 19- March 20)

Pisces is one of the most sensitive signs in the Zodiac. Many people also find it difficult to understand them. Pisces at their best can be creative and compassionate. They are natural observers and like to take the back seat most of the time.

Pisces Man

Pisces always find itself in between reality and the world of spiritualism. They are often gentle, affectionate ad sensitive to other's emotions. They are also very friendly and compassionate. Pisces men like to share their thoughts with like like-minded peers.

- Be sensitive and gentle. Unlike other fiery men, a Pisces male tends to be more gentle and nurturing. They like to explore your natural sensitivity and vulnerability.

- Get in touch with your creative side. Pisces men are always in touch with their creative side and tend to look for women who like to express their creativity.

- Get along with his friends and family. Pisces tends to value their friends and family very much and one way to attract him is to make an effort to get along with the people that are important in his life.

Pisces Woman

Pisces women are mysterious and romantic who rely on their deep emotions. They can also be very imaginative and creative. Most women born under this sign have the inclination for performing arts, writing and music.

- Make the first move. Even if she likes you, a Pisces woman will rarely make the first move. Make a move but avoid coming on too strong. A simple hello and a smile can already capture her attention.

- Be adventurous. A Pisces likes to learn new things and meet new people. Taking her out for an adventure will give you an opportunity to learn more things about her.

- Open up to her. She would want to know everything about her partner. They do not aim to control anyone but would want to be able to see the world through different eyes.

Best Love Matches

Scorpio

Pisces and Scorpio can feel mutual affection for each other immediately. Scorpio will naturally assume control over the relationship and Pisces will be more than happy to give it to them. Both signs also share the same interest over the unknown and unusual.

Cancer

Cancer and Pisces are both very sensitive so they make a good match. Pisces will bask in the protective nature of Cancer while Pisces dreaminess will be good for Cancer.

Capricorn

Capricorn and Pisces are two different signs but they can complement each other well. The practical Capricorn can guide Pisces into the right direction. Capricorn will also benefit from Pisces' imagination.

Conclusion

Thank you again for downloading this book!

I hope this book was able to help you to understand zodiac relationship.

The next step is to try these tips yourself.

Finally, if you enjoyed this book, please take the time to share your thoughts and post a review on Amazon. It'd be greatly appreciated!

Thank you and good luck!